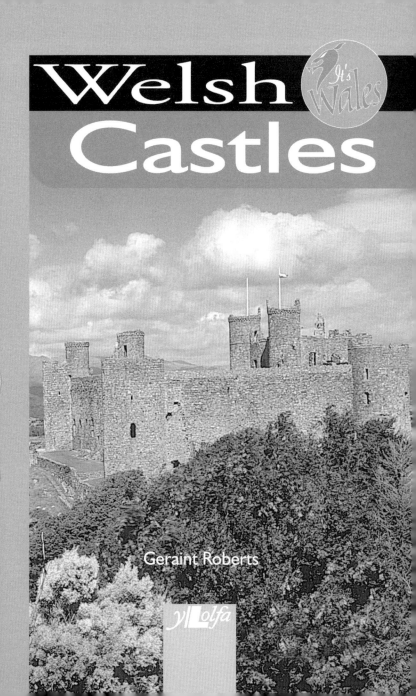

Welsh
Castles

It's Wales

Geraint Roberts

y Lolfa

First impression: 2001
© Copyright Geraint Roberts and Y Lolfa Cyf., 2001

Thanks to the Wales Tourist Board for the Photographs.
Cover design: Ceri Jones

ISBN: 0 86243 550 1

Printed on acid free and partly recycled paper
and published and bound in Wales by:
Y Lolfa Cyf., Talybont, Ceredigion SY24 5AP
e-mail ylolfa@ylolfa.com
internet www.ylolfa.com
phone +44 (0)1970 832 304
fax 832 782
isdn 832 813

Contents

Introduction

This is not a guidebook that meticulously details the entire course of a castle's history and explains minutely how its fortifications developed over the years. Most of the fortresses that have been included have their own, specific, guidebooks, often published by the old Ministry of Works or Cadw: Welsh Historic Monuments. Nor is it a gazetteer of all Wales's castles and fortifications – a number of excellent surveys of this sort are available and are detailed in the bibliography.

This book is an attempt to tell some of the stories that are to be found in the past of many of Wales's castles. It deals more with the people that dwelt within or in the shadow of the castle walls than the buildings, the wood, masonry and earth that in times past sheltered its inhabitants. Some are stories of war and bloodshed, whilst others are in a slightly more peaceful vein, but all reflect the rich history of Wales. All stories are either set within or near the castle, or concern someone closely associated with it. Some stories are well-documented fact, but others are, perhaps, legends that have been associated with the castle over the years.

These events are set in a factual framework that will enhance the reader's understanding. The relevant periods of Welsh history are briefly surveyed, as is the development of fortifications over time.

As these events took place so long ago, evidence is often sparse or conflicting. In the event of any confusion over facts or dates, I have attempted to follow those found in the volumes of the *Oxford History of Wales* series wherever possible.

Bear in mind that castles can be dangerous places. There may be no-one shooting arrows or dropping rocks from the battlements today (unless you're very unlucky), but a fall from crumbling masonry or down a steep bank can be just as deadly! Castles can be wonderful places to excite the imagination of children, especially if they hear about the dramatic events that took place there centuries ago. Children must be supervised, however, and made aware of the potential dangers that may be found in many old buildings such as castles.

Please check that castles are open before going. Some of these buildings lie on private land. The owner's permission must be sought before visiting these. If a castle lies on or near farmland, please follow the Countryside code, closing gates behind you and keeping dogs on a lead. Some castles offer added attractions at certain times during the year, such as re-creations of events that happened nearby, or of the life of castle dwellers in the past. The prospective visitor might check with the castle itself or the press for details.

The exploration of castles can be a fascinating and rewarding hobby. The reader in search of more information is referred to the book list, where reference is made to further, often more detailed, works. It is hoped that this brief survey may enhance enjoyment of these amazing places, fire the imagination, and inspire more people to visit and to discover more about the castles of Wales.

Castles in Welsh History

It is often said that Wales is a land of castles. Indeed, as we shall see, Wales has the highest proportion of castles per square mile in the world. As people have always wanted a safe place to live, the construction of buildings that could be defended against an aggressor is a strong thread that runs through the history of Wales. This book will attempt to trace the development of defensive structures in Wales, focusing particularly on those which we call 'castles', and will also attempt to explain their context – why there was such a need to provide secure living spaces in the first place.

We shall also learn more about the people and events associated with some of them. This introduction can only be a brief summary of Welsh history. More detailed accounts may be found in the bibliography.

One can hardly travel more than a few miles in Wales before coming across a defensive structure. The earliest of such structures that can be seen today are the hillforts, enclosures constructed on the tops of hills or mountains. Some of these are now known to date back to the late Bronze Age – perhaps around 1000 BC. These structures may often have been built by the Celts, and are known as *oppida*.

They may well have acted as a focal point for the number of tribes that inhabited Europe. Whilst many are strongly fortified, not all are: some do not appear to be primarily military structures. A number of the Welsh *oppida* are impressive – stone-built Tre'r Ceiri on the Llŷn peninsula, Pendinas above Aberystwyth and Dinas Brân near Llangollen, for example.

They were certainly focal points of native resistance to the invading Romans. Julius Caesar describes the native British fortifications that he and his legions came across during their second invasion of Britain in 54 BC: '…a well-fortified post of great natural strength,' he wrote, '…previously prepared, no doubt, for some war amongst themselves, since all the entrances were blocked by felled trees laid close together.' He goes on to mention more native strongholds: '…densely wooded spots fortified with a rampart and trench…' Needless to say, for Caesar at least, these places were not nearly strong enough to withstand Roman grit and steel.

Graphic evidence of Roman attacks has been discovered at Maiden Castle in Dorset in the shape of skeletons bearing wounds obviously inflicted by Roman weapons. A particularly striking example is that of a ballista bolt found embedded in the spine of one of the unfortunate defenders.

The Romans themselves built many forts in their conquered territories, often choosing fine defensive positions which drew later castle builders to the same sites – Cardiff is a good example of this.

By the fourth century Roman rule in Britain was far from stable. Many Roman troops left Britain with Magnus Maximus when he left to press his claims as Emperor in 383 AD. Maximus is known in Welsh as Macsen Wledig, and features in the tale from the *Mabinogi,* 'Breuddwyd Macsen', or 'Macsen's Dream'. Britain was left poorly defended, and by around 410 there was no longer an official Roman presence in Britain.

The succeeding years were anxious ones for the Britons, many of whom had become Romanized and Christian, as waves of foreign invaders attacked and colonised their eastern lands in what is now England. These invaders included the Germanic Angles, Saxons and Jutes, who drove many Britons westwards and northwards. This was the time that Arthur is said to have resisted the pagan Anglo-Saxon advance, although his existence is far from certain. What is certain is that the Saxons ultimately succeeded in establishing themselves in most of what is now England, with British controlled enclaves in modern Cornwall, Wales and Southern Scotland.

The dispossessed Britons took to calling themselves 'Cymry' – 'Comrades' or 'Fellow-countrymen' – and gave their names to some of their territories: Cumbria in what is now northern England, and 'Cymru' or Wales. The Anglo-Saxons called them *wealas,* or foreigners. This word was later to become 'Welsh', and they thus became foreigners in what had until recently been their own lands.

There were undoubtedly defensive enclosures in Wales during this time, but there was nothing that may be correctly described as a 'Castle' until just before the Norman invasion which began in 1066. A castle may be defined as the private fortress of a king, or of a noble, and was a product of the feudal system. Defensive enclosures in Early Medieval Britain, including Anglo-Saxon *burhs* which were enclosed villages or towns, tended to be more communal.

Edward the Confessor, Saxon king of England, had spent much time in Normandy, and brought some Norman favourites over with him. They erected some early castles in the troublesome borderlands or Marches between England and Wales, but within a few years many more were to be built.

William I, conqueror of England, built a castle almost as soon as he landed in the country in 1066. It was of the simple motte and bailey design, and served as a base from which the surrounding countryside could be pacified, and a refuge if superior forces attacked. This castle is depicted on the Bayeux Tapestry that tells William's story.

The Normans turned their attentions to Wales fairly quickly. They needed to secure their western borders, and a number of land-hungry knights wanted to carve territories out for themselves by force. They attacked along the easier land of the river valleys and avoided the inhospitable uplands wherever possible, as the Welsh could employ their guerrilla tactics effectively in their native mountains. On the flat, however, the heavily-armed and armoured Normans on their war-horses had a distinct advantage and proved to be formidable soldiers.

From 1067 William Fitzosbern used Hereford as his base for incursions into south-east Wales. By 1071 Roger of Montgomery was based at Shrewsbury, and Hugh 'the Wolf' of Avranches had his headquarters at Chester. The three were created earls, and had virtually royal powers within the lands that they won with their swords. This pattern of independent 'Marcher lordships' was to persist for centuries, until the Acts of Union with England in 1536-42.

The Welsh at this time were ruled by many small local kings, princes or lords. This meant that if one lord's territory was captured, or he himself was killed or captured by the invaders, the neighbouring Welsh rulers could continue their rule. The more centralised Saxon kingdom fell at virtually a stroke when Harold II died at Hastings. It took the Normans, who could later be described as English, much longer to capture Wales.

The Welsh were congenitally quarrelsome, however, and were constantly fighting amongst themselves. The Welsh system of land inheritance also led to a lack of continuity as a father's lands were traditionally divided up amongst his sons, rather than passing virtually intact to one heir as in the Norman and English system. Brother fought against brother for control of a lordship, and then frequently turned on neighbouring rulers in search of more land or power. This can be seen time and again in medieval Wales – Llywelyn ap Gruffudd of Gwynedd in north-west Wales, was forever struggling against his brothers Dafydd, Rhodri and Owain, who was in fact the eldest son. There was thus little prospect of a Welsh united front developing, and the Normans were to conquer the country piecemeal. Interestingly, it has been argued that a consistent pattern may be seen in these inter-feuds, with one of the parties involved in each feud turning to the Normans or English for support against the other party, which may be described as being more pro-Welsh.

Hugh of Avranches and his men made inroads into North Wales, taking land as far west as Anglesey and Caernarfon. Rhys ap Tewdwr, ruler of Deheubarth or south-west Wales, fell in battle in 1093 and Normans poured in to the South. Bernard of Neufmarché took much of Brycheiniog or Brecknock, the de Braoses moved into Radnor and Robert Fitzhammo conquered much of Glamorgan. All of these conquerors erected castles of the simple motte and bailey type that were their bases as they subjugated the surrounding lands. An example of this may be seen in the chapter on Pembroke castle.

There was perhaps only one stone castle in Wales during this initial period, where the mighty keep at Chepstow was built in stone by Fitzosbern, but as the twelfth century wore on stone became more common, often replacing older timber defences.

Some Welsh rulers succeeded in building up a substantial power base. Owain Gwynedd (1137–70) was the dominant force in the North West, and Rhys ap Gruffudd (1132–97) or '*Yr Arglwydd Rhys*' the Lord Rhys, in Deheubarth. Both men learnt to emulate Norman tactics. It seems that Rhys may have numbered armoured horsemen among his soldiers, for example, whereas the Welsh were traditionally foot soldiers, spearmen or bowmen. Gerald of Wales (see Pembroke Castle), who travelled across Wales in 1188, described the conduct of Welshmen in battle. They were very ferocious when battle was first joined, he said, but were thrown into confusion if they did not make early breakthroughs, and were quick to run away if things did not go well!

Carreg Cennen in Carmarthenshire, one of the strongholds of Lord Rhys in the 12th century.

The more successful Welsh rulers, such as Rhys and Owain, realised that they should also adopt the use of castles. Native-built castles therefore began to join the many Norman fortifications that littered the countryside. The Welsh also captured and held Norman-built fortresses against their erstwhile owners, and sometimes improved the defences. It should also be noted that Rhys and Owain were willing to attack fellow Welsh rulers at times, and that Welshman often fought against Welshman, sometimes in alliance with the Norman invaders.

Gwynedd was to become the dominant native Welsh territory. Llywelyn ap Iorwerth (1173–1240) built up his power in Gwynedd, becoming known as *Llywelyn Fawr*, Llywelyn the Great. He was to build a number of castles (see Dolwyddelan) and extend his influence beyond the boundaries of his territory, but not all Welsh lords were his allies. His death saw the eventual fragmenting of his lands as Welsh and what may now be described as the English, rather than the Norman, lords fought over the pieces.

His grandson Llywelyn ap Gruffudd (c.1225–82) recovered much of his grandfather's land and influence but was to fall to a force of English and pressed Welsh troops led by Edward I, the English king (see Dolforwyn, Castell y Bere, and Aberedw and Builth castles). Llywelyn is known to the Welsh as '*ein Llyw Olaf*', our last leader. Following his death, Edward I built a series of magnificent and intimidating castles across North and Mid Wales in an attempt to over-awe and dominate the fractious natives. He also founded a number of boroughs or towns such as Conwy and Caernarfon in the shadow of these castles, bringing in English settlers. The Statute of Rhuddlan of 1284 enshrined Edward's policy towards Wales and proclaimed its annexation to the English state.

English power expanded despite occasional Welsh uprisings (see Caerffili and Dryslwyn castles). The next serious Welsh challenge to English power was led by Owain Glyndŵr (*c.*1154–*c.*1415). A Welsh lord or *uchelwr* (gentleman), who had the blood of the princes of both North and South Wales in his veins, Glyndŵr rose up against the English in 1400. He was to have many successes, taking a number of English castles (see Sycharth and Harlech castles), and it has been said that at the height of his success only the network of English-held castles stood between Glyndŵr and the complete overthrow of English power in Wales. Eventually, however, his forces succumbed to superior English wealth and power and Glyndŵr disappeared. He may have died at his daughter's home in what is now Herefordshire, but this is not known for certain.

What are now known as the Wars of the Roses in England and Wales began in 1455, and were brought to and end in 1485 when Henry Tudor, descendant of an Anglesey family, landed his troops at Haverfordwest and marched into England with a mainly Welsh army (see Kidwelly Castle). King Richard III was killed at Bosworth Field, Henry was crowned king as Henry VII, and many Welshmen took service under the new Tudor dynasty.

Wales and England became more peaceful and landowners often abandoned uncomfortable old castles in favour of fortified manor houses and later more luxurious country houses. Castles were to be important once again, however, when struggles between King Charles I and Parliament resulted in the English Revolution or Civil War. This was in fact two wars – the first from 1642 to 1647, and the second in 1648. Charles was beheaded in 1649, and Britain became a Commonwealth. Oliver Cromwell was Lord Protector from 1653 to 1658. His feeble son Richard could not hold on to power and in 1660 Charles II, son of the executed Charles I, returned to rule.

Many castles had been slighted, or demolished, following the Revolution so that they could not be used militarily, and the age of the castle effectively came to an end in Britain. Castles were either abandoned – which often meant that they became 'quarries' for building stone – or adapted to become more comfortable dwellings. Ironically, later country houses such as those at Craig y Nos near Ystradgynlais in the Tawe valley and Penrhyn near Bangor in Gwynedd were sometimes given mock battlements and turrets as such things became fashionable. Some medieval castles were 'restored', the efforts of the Marquesses of Bute at Cardiff Castle (see the relevant chapter) and Castell Coch being spectacular examples of 19th-20th century interpretations of what a castle 'should' look like.

Although they no longer fulfil their original purpose, castles still dominate much of Wales. Hundreds of castles, whether massive and imposing stone strongholds or barely visible earthworks, dot the countryside. Wales can justly be called a land of castles, and their study casts much light on the country's history.

The Development of the Castle

The castle as brought to Britain by the Normans was essentially a simple structure. A wooden tower was built upon a natural or artificial mound or motte, with a wooden palisade surrounding a courtyard or bailey underneath, which in turn was surrounded by a moat or dry ditch which had provided material from which the motte was built up. Stables, halls and other domestic apartments were sited in the bailey. Sometimes there would be more than one bailey, or even another motte, but the essential elements were the same. An example of such a castle may be seen on the Bayeux Tapestry.

These were quick, cheap and easy to build, but were vulnerable to sustained attacks, especially if fire was used against the timber structures. Wood also rotted, of course, leaving many simple earthworks where once there was a wooden castle – Trecastle in Powys is a good example of this.

Stone was stronger and more durable, but more expensive and more difficult to work. Stone structures sometimes replace wooden ones – the wooden gatehouse, perhaps, or the keep or central tower that was the last refuge if the outer curtain walls and towers fell. The keep was also known as the donjon, and sometimes held prisoners, which gives us the word 'dungeon'. A stone keep was sometimes too heavy for an artificial mound and would have subsided or collapsed, so sometimes a shell keep was built on its summit. This was a stone wall, which enclosed the top of the mound, and which had wooden rooms inside it. This was lighter than a solid stone construction. An example may be seen at Cardiff.

Alternatively, a larger solid stone keep could be built, and many were from the 11th century onwards. The White Tower at the Tower of London was an early example and was started during the reign of William I, the Conqueror. Early examples were square or rectangular, but this made them more vulnerable to assaults on the corners that gave a better target for bombardment, battering or undermining.

Castle defences developed as a result of attempts to stay one step ahead of the besiegers. Several siege engines were available to the medieval attacker. The mangonel was a catapult that used twisted rope or fibre to hurl stones or other missiles. A more powerful catapult, the trebuchet, was powered by a heavy counterweight at the end of the beam that held the missile. Massive stones could be thrown at defenders or walls, and even dead animals could be catapulted over the walls in an attempt to spread disease. Attackers could also try to starve defenders out, or hope that they would run out of water or succumb to the diseases that could spread like wildfire in the stifling atmosphere of a castle under siege. Siege towers or belfries could be built of wood and rolled towards the castle walls, or scaling ladders could be employed. Attackers would try to overwhelm the defenders on the parapet, whilst the defenders might try to topple the ladder or belfry, or set the belfry alight despite the animal hides soaked in water which often covered them. Walls could also be built higher, of course, although this was more expensive and technically more difficult.

If the castle wall was undermined – square corners being particularly vulnerable – and the tunnel filled with brushwood and set alight, the resulting gap under the foundations might cause the wall to collapse. This could backfire, as at the siege of Dryslwyn in 1287. The defenders might also dig a counter-tunnel and attempt to drive the attacking miners back in a vicious subterranean fight. A battering ram could be used against foundations or gates, but this had to cross the moat or ditch if there was one. The wielders of the ram would also be under attack.

Defenders naturally wanted to be able to fight back against besiegers, so a number of innovations were introduced. The top of walls was crenellated, or provided with the distinctive blocks of masonry behind which defenders could shelter. Arrows and other missiles could be projected through machicolations, or holes in the floor of the parapet along the top of the wall, or through arrow loops in the wall itself. Similar openings inside passages were known as murder holes. Covered wooden galleries or hoardings could be built out over the parapet, which also enabled defenders to drop rocks and other unpleasant surprises on those below, although these were rare in Britain. The bottom of walls could be splayed out, both to strengthen the structure and to cause dropped missiles to rebound upon besiegers in interesting and unpredictable ways.

Round keeps and D-shaped towers that presented a rounded face to the attacker became popular. Like the rectangular keeps, they were usually surrounded by curtain walls and towers. The enclosed space was known as a bailey or ward. Gatehouses were vulnerable, and became very large and impressive. They sometimes became formidable enough to take the place of the keep as the final refuge, as at Harlech Castle. During the 13th century another, lower wall was sometimes added around the inner wall. This meant that missiles could be projected from both walls, and if the outer wall was taken the attackers still had another formidable obstacle facing them. These were known as concentric castles, and perhaps the finest example is that at Beaumaris in Anglesey. This was one of the magnificent fortresses built by Edward I to dominate and pacify North Wales after the fall of Llywelyn ap Gruffudd in 1282. Not all were concentric, sometimes because the shape of the site would not allow it, but all were extremely formidable. Some were to fall because of trickery, such as at Conwy in 1401 when Owain Glyndŵr's men gained entry by pretending to be carpenters.

However, a threat to the supremacy of castles was developing. Gunpowder technology was improving, and heavy cannon were employed. Cannon existed in 1326, and by around 1380 gunports were built into walls, for example, at Canterbury Westgate in Kent. Heavier cannon could batter walls with great effectiveness. Castles became less effective.

Castles played a major part during the 15th century Glyndŵr war and the Wars of the Roses, but successive monarchs cut down the power of the great nobles and disbanded private armies prior to the Acts of Union between Wales and England in 1536-42. Castles were not just less effective, they were not necessary in a more peaceful country. Great landowners built more comfortable homes which became less and less defensible, whilst less illustrious gentry built fortified manor houses, which were more comfortable than draughty old castles but were still defensible in times of trouble. Defence gradually ceased to become much of a concern. Many castles were abandoned or adapted to become more modern dwellings

The last hurrah of the castle in England and Wales came during the English Revolution or Civil War in the mid 17th century, when many old fortifications were held for king or Parliament, and perhaps many a gentleman regretted abandoning the safety of his ancestral stronghold for a flimsy des. res.

Following the Revolution many castles were slighted or demolished, and many fell into decay. The age of the castle was effectively over.

Pembroke *Penfro*

Pembroke Castle, 12th century.

Gerald of Wales was an Anglo-Welsh churchman who has left us a vivid picture of Welsh life in the 12th century. He was the son of a Welsh mother and a Norman father, and spent much of his life endeavouring, unsuccessfully, to become Bishop of St David's. He travelled through Wales with the Archbishop of Canterbury in an attempt to recruit Crusaders in 1188, and recorded his experiences in his *Journey through Wales*.

His journey took him to Pembroke, a place where, Gerald relates, Arnulf de Montgomery built the first castle from wood and timber during the reign of Henry I. Gerald is wrong here, for the first castle at the site was built c.1091, during the reign of William Rufus, Henry I's brother. Arnulf returned to England, leaving Gerald of Windsor and a small garrison to defend the castle.

The local Welsh, sensing a chance to cast out the Norman invaders, laid siege to the castle, which seems to have been a motte and bailey. The siege lasted for quite some time, and things became desperate within the wooden walls – so desperate that fifteen Norman knights deserted one night under cover of darkness. Gerald of Windsor, enraged, transferred their estates to fifteen of his own men at arms, dubbing them knights on the spot.

Food was scarce, but Gerald tricked the Welsh besiegers into believing the garrison still well-provisioned by taunting them from the walls, and throwing some of his last supplies – four hogs – over the castle walls. He also arranged for a letter, signed with his own seal, supposedly to Arnulf and claiming that the garrison would need no reinforcements for another four months.

Gerald of Wales, who was, incidentally, Gerald of Windsor's grandson, claims that the gullible Welsh were completely taken in and lifted the siege, departing in despair. First round to granddad, and well done the Normans.

Gerald goes on to relate some other interesting stories set in Pembroke castle, tales of murder, torture, and of a grief-stricken, maternal weasel. A man discovered her kittens in a sheepskin in the castle. He removed them to a safe place and waited for the mother's return. Devastated at her loss, she spat venom into a jug of milk intended for the man's son. Seeing this, the man returned the kittens. The mother's relief was all too plain, says Gerald, as she rushed back to the milk jug and knocked it over. Her gratitude for the return of her babies meant that she was determined that her host's son should suffer no harm.

Many other stories that shed much light on the author's life and times may be found in Gerald's *Journey through Wales* and *Description of Wales*.

The present castle is an impressive building, set on a rocky site, which, due to its steep sides and formidable defences, was virtually impregnable. The massive, late 12th century round keep is regarded as the finest example of its type in the British Isles. There is a large cavern, known as the Wogan, beneath one of the two halls adjoining the outer curtain wall.

Pembroke is a very impressive fortification, with well-produced and informative exhibitions, and is well worth a visit.

Abergavenny *Y Fenni*

Near Abergavenny town centre, Monmouthshire.

This was the castle of William de Braose, a man who earned himself an unenviable reputation for cruelty throughout Wales and the Marches. The curtain walls which remain were probably built by de Braose, whilst the great hall and gatehouse are later, from the 13th to 15th centuries.

These curtain walls, then, probably stood during one of the most notorious acts of treachery in the long and bitter struggles for land and power between the native Welsh and incoming Normans. Gwent, the area in which this castle was built, was one of the areas that saw most tension between the Welsh and the invaders.

In the late 12th century one of the most prominent Welsh leaders in Gwent was Seisyll ap Dyfnwal. In 1175 Seisyll killed Henry, son of the Earl of Hereford. Henry had been, briefly, Lord of Breconshire, including Abergavenny. When Henry's brother Mahel was killed by a falling stone during a fire at the nearby castle of Bronllys, their relative William de Braose succeeded to the lordship.

Late in 1175 de Braose invited Seisyll, his son Geoffrey, and many other Welshmen, to celebrate Christmas with him at the castle. The Welshmen suspected nothing and came unarmed to the Norman lord's stronghold. During the feasting the Normans set upon their guests, killing every one. De Braose's men then attacked Seisyll's fortress, Castell Arnallt, destroying it and murdering Seisyll's wife and young son Cadwaladr.

This base act of treachery echoed an earlier event in the 5th century, '*Brad y Cyllyll Hirion*', the Treason of the Long Knives, a similar massacre of Welshmen by the Saxons of Hengest and Horsa many centuries before (see Dinas Emrys). Certainly the local Welsh were outraged by de Braose's infamous behaviour.

Seven years later, according to Gerald of Wales (see Pembroke Castle), Welsh forces stormed Abergavenny. The Welsh attackers, sons and grandsons of de Braose's murder victims, scaled the walls on ladders and captured the constable and his wife. They then 'burned the whole place down,' says Gerald. So, maintains the chronicler, 'God in his justice thus decreed that the original crime should be punished on the very spot where it had been committed.'

Soon after, the avenging Welshmen attacked Ranulf Poer, Sheriff of Herefordshire, and his men as they were building a castle at Dingestow near Monmouth. Ranulf, nine of the leading Norman captains of Gwent, and many of his men were killed. William de Braose was captured, but was quickly rescued and lived to pursue his conquests.

Following these bloody events, said the chronicler of *Brut y Tywysogion*, the Chronicle of the Welsh Princes, 'none of the Welsh dared place their trust in the French'. They had good reason. In 1197 another Welsh leader, Trahaearn Fychan, was seized on his way to de Braose's court. Trahaearn was taken to Brecon, dragged through the town at the tail of a horse, and beheaded. His body was hung upside down on the gallows for three days.

Incidentally, it was during the siege of Abergavenny Castle that an arrow from a Welsh bow penetrated the oaken castle door, a mighty feat which was often quoted to prove the power of Welsh bows and bowmen.

The castle in Kidwelly, Carmarthenshire.

The first castle on this site was built in 1106 by Roger, Bishop of Salisbury, who also established the nearby town. Medieval bishops were powerful landowners and lords in their own right, with many not averse to taking to the battlefield on occasion. Some of them got round a Biblical injunction that clergy should not use the sword by wielding a mace or battleaxe instead, thus fulfilling the letter if not the spirit of the scripture.

Bishop Roger chose his site well, as it could be supplied by sea and controlled the river Gwendraeth beneath the steep ridge upon which it was built. The first castle was built in wood, and rebuilt by Rhys ap Gruffudd c.1190/6. By the 13th century the de Chaworth family rebuilt it in stone whilst following the distinctive bow-shaped outline of the wooden defences. After further additions it was eventually to become concentric in plan and had a particularly fine gatehouse at the southern end of the castle. This held both domestic apartments and refinements such as murder holes through which missiles and rocks could be poured upon the unfortunate attackers.

The last refinements were added to this castle by Sir Rhys ap Thomas around the turn of the 16th century. Rhys, a prominent supporter of Henry VII and the Tudors, was knighted following the battle of Bosworth. His improvements again added to the domestic comforts of the castle, but it was virtually ruined by the 17th century as fashions changed and comfort took precedence over defensive capabilities. Long before Sir Rhys became lord, however, one of his countrywomen had played a major part in a drama enacted nearby in 1136.

She was Gwenllïan, daughter of Gruffudd ap Cynan, king of Gwynedd, and wife of Gruffudd ap Rhys, lord of Deheubarth. Gwenllïan was no shrinking violet, and showed that women could often attain prominent roles in Welsh society.

During a time of trouble in this area, Gruffudd her husband went to ask his father-in-law for reinforcements. Gwenllïan raised an army in his absence and led them forth against a force led by Geoffrey, the Bishop's steward, and Maurice de Londres, a Norman who was to become lord of Kidwelly and its castle when the redoubtable Roger died.

Gwenllïan was, says the ever-informative Gerald of Wales, like Penthesilea, Queen of the Amazons. She had been so sure of victory that she brought two of her sons with her. One of them, Morgan, was killed, and the other, Maelgwn, was captured. Gwenllïan and many of her followers were beheaded on the battlefield, still known as *Maes Gwenllïan*, Gwenllïan's Field, to this day.

Her husband Gruffudd succeeded in winning his lands back from the Normans, but he was dead within a year. He had not been a particularly powerful ruler, but one of his and Gwenllïan's sons, Rhys, was to make his mark upon the history of Wales. Rhys was just four or five years of age at the time of his mother's death, but was eventually to become ruler of Deheubarth in his own right, and to become known as *Yr Arglwydd Rhys*, the Lord Rhys (see Cardigan). Kidwelly Castle was to be a constant thorn in his side. Rhys and one of his sons, Rhys Gryg, were both to capture and hold Kidwelly Castle on separate occasions, although both were to lose control after a time.

Maurice de Londres was a simple man according to Gerald of Wales. This may be an euphemistic way of saying that Maurice was not the cleverest knight in the castle. He was very fond and protective of the deer which he owned, although this perhaps owed more to his own desire to keep them safe until he hunted them than to any early inclination towards wildlife conservation. His wife played a trick on him in collusion with their shepherds and other servants. She claimed that her husband's deer were in fact savage beasts, and had been running wild and viciously attacking his sheep. Two stags were produced, which proved to have their intestines stuffed with wool. The 'simple' Maurice was thoroughly taken in, and set his hounds on the deer forthwith. A simple man, who obviously believed in straightforward solutions to the problems which faced him.

Cardiff *Caerdydd*

Cardiff Castle, in the city centre

Cardiff Castle's impressive fortifications are well known to the thousands that flock to the Welsh capital to shop or to watch rugby. The curtain wall is, indeed, very impressive, although much is the Victorian 'reconstruction' created by the coal-owning aristocrat, the Marquess of Bute, and by William Burgess, his architect.

It is, however, a very old site. It actually occupies the area of a Roman fort, and the remains of this structure, discovered in the 18th century, were built into the later reconstruction. The invading Normans appreciated its strategic value and also took advantage of the site, initially building a wooden motte and bailey. These were succeeded by a stone shell keep and curtain walls, and later by stronger towers.

It was in 1158, during a period of ownership by William de Clare, Earl of Gloucester, that the castle was taken by storm by Ifor ap Meurig, Welsh lord of Senghennydd to the north of Cardiff. He was known as *Ifor Bach* or Little Ifor. Gerald of Wales, to whom we are indebted for the following story, describes him as being 'a man of immense courage, but very short.'

William de Clare was trying to take Ifor's land away from him – something that Ifor naturally resented as he, his family and fellow Welsh people felt that they had already lost enough to the Norman invaders.

The castle was defended by very high walls, says Gerald, and was garrisoned by at least one hundred and twenty men at arms and many archers. Furthermore, Cardiff was packed with de Clare's supporters.

Ifor, nothing daunted, carried ladders to the walls, climbed them, seized the Earl, his wife, and their only son, and made good his escape into his native woods. These woods extended as far south as what are now the northern suburbs of Cardiff – Whitchurch and Rhiwbeina. This escapade did not reflect well on the Normans, and particularly on the vigilance of their sentries.

Ifor then refused to release his hostages until he had recovered everything that had been stolen from him, and a little more besides. This was a rare example of a Welshman gaining recompense and compensation from one of the Norman or English invaders.

Ifor's name lives on in Cardiff's Welsh language club, Clwb Ifor Bach in Womanby Street, appropriately enough a stone's throw from the castle that could not keep him and his men out. This is as good a place to go as any, after Ivor's successors have defeated the English once more, albeit on the rugby field this time. If by some mischance the Welsh come second, comfort can at least be taken in the exploits of the brave lord of Senghennydd in 1158.

Cardigan *Aberteifi*

Remains of the castle in Cardigan, Ceredigion.

Two castles are known here. Cardigan Old Castle, about a mile south-east of the modern town, was built by Roger of Montgomery in 1093. Very little now remains. The second castle which lies in the modern town may well have been built by Rhys ap Gruffudd, known as 'yr Arglwydd Rhys' or 'the Lord Rhys', perhaps around 1170. He certainly had a castle here at that time.

Rhys was the lord of Deheubarth and a contemporary of Owain Gwynedd, the northern prince. Rhys had to deal with the old problem that beset Welsh lords and princes – trying to fight off or negotiate with his fellow Welsh lords, English nobles and the English king. It was not an easy task, but he achieved some success.

After coming under considerable pressure from Henry II of England, his large land holdings in west Wales were confirmed by 1171, and he received the title of Justiciar of South Wales from the king. He had a large family, and married his children off to many influential South Wales families, thus creating a number of valuable alliances and connections. He also built or held many castles, including those at Rhayader, Dinefwr, Cilgerran, and so on. It may be that Rhys's castle at Cardigan was the first stone-built Welsh castle.

Although he worked closely with the English king and nobles, Rhys was a Welshman above all. This was a time when musicians, and especially poets, travelled around the courts of Welsh lords and princes, often praising their patrons in poetry and song in return for hospitality. Rhys took his role as a patron of the traditional poetic and musical arts seriously, and is credited with patronising the first *Eisteddfod*, or musical and poetic competition. The story may be found in *Brut y Tywysogion*, or the 'Chronicle of the Welsh Princes'.

Over Christmas 1176 Rhys held a magnificent court in his castle at Cardigan. This festival had been announced a year before, throughout Wales, England, Scotland, Ireland and other islands. Two types of competition were held there – one for poets, and one for musicians. Harpers, crowders (who played the *crwth* or crowd, a type of bowed string instrument traditional to Wales), and pipers competed for the musical prize.

Two chairs were awarded, one each to the victorious poet and musician. A young man from Rhys's own court was the leading harper, whilst a man of Gwynedd won the poetry chair.

Rhys was open-handed and generous to all, says the *Brut*. This must have been a splendid occasion.

This, then, is often quoted as the first *Eisteddfod*. Nowadays there are many local *Eisteddfodau* throughout Wales, including special ones held for young people by the *Urdd*, or Welsh League of Youth. The National Eisteddfod is held alternately in North or South Wales, and is one of the largest cultural festivals in Europe.

Rhys ap Gruffudd himself was to hold the reins of power in the south until his death in 1197, by which time he had been fighting and negotiating for over sixty years. He had been the dominant Welsh prince for some forty of those years. Unfortunately, and entirely predictably, following his death internal squabbles led to the decline of his dynasty and presaged even more splits and infighting between the native Welsh lords. The Welsh, it seemed, would never learn to keep a united front. Some would argue that this is still the case.

Cardigan Castle is now much decayed, and in private hands.

Dinas Emrys

Near Beddgelert, 12 miles south-east of Caernarfon, Gwynedd.

This castle stands near the town of Beddgelert, famed as the burial place of Gelert, the faithful hound of prince Llywelyn ap Iorwerth (see Dolwyddelan). Gelert defended his master's baby son from a wolf when Llywelyn went out hunting, but when the prince returned he saw the bloodstained bedclothes but could not see his son – or the body of the wolf. Gelert had the wolf's blood all over his jaws. Llywelyn jumped to the wrong conclusion and killed the hound. Soon after he found his son safe and well, and discovered the slain wolf. Llywelyn became grief-stricken when he discovered his error and buried his dog nearby. Beddgelert means 'Gelert's grave'.

Of course those who claim that the landlord of a nearby hotel invented this popular story a couple of centuries ago, and that Gelert was an ancient Welsh saint, could perhaps be dismissed as spoilsports.

The remains of Dinas Emrys Castle are in a very poor condition. It was probably built by the Welsh at the beginning of the 13th century, although there seems to be no contemporary reference to the medieval castle. The site is naturally very strong and defensible, and the 13th century defences were not the first to take advantage of the site.

According to Geoffrey of Monmouth, the somewhat unreliable twelfth century chronicler, Gwrtheyrn or Vortigern, king of the Britons, built the first fortress at Dinas Emrys. It was Vortigern who invited Hengest, Horsa and their Saxon followers to Britain just after the Romans left the British Isles for good. Soon after, the Saxons betrayed the Britons, murdering most of the British leaders at a feast. This massacre became known as *Brad y Cyllyll Hirion*, the Treason of the Long Knives (see Abergavenny).

The Britons were driven northwards and westwards to their lands in what is now northern England, southern Scotland, Wales and Cornwall. Eventually the Britons were to be known as the Welsh, from the Anglo-Saxon word '*wealas*', or foreigners. The dispossessed Welsh thus became foreigners in what had been their own lands.

When he saw the devastation he had brought upon his people, Vortigern retreated into Gwynedd. Here, at Dinas Emrys, he decided to build a castle. However, the walls that were built during the day were swallowed up by the earth by the next morning. Vortigern's magicians told him that he must find a boy without a father, kill him, and sprinkle his blood on the stones and mortar so that the walls would remain standing.

Such a boy was found in Carmarthen. His mother, a princess of Dyfed, confessed that her son's father was in fact a demon who had seduced her, and that her son was therefore fatherless.

The boy's name was Myrddin, or Merlin. Being understandably eager to avoid the knife, he told the king that the magicians were wrong. The walls would not stand firm because a pool lay beneath them. In the pool were two dragons, white and red. Vortigern ordered that this be investigated. When the pool was drained, the dragons attacked each other and fought viciously before the king and his companions.

Vortigern asked Merlin what this meant. The boy told him that the Red Dragon represented the people of Britain, whilst the White Dragon represented the invading Saxons. Eventually the Red Dragon would overcome the White. Merlin made a number of other prophecies, but this particular prophecy was to be held dear by the Welsh for centuries, foretelling as it did the eventual triumph of the Welsh over the invaders.

Merlin, of course, was to go on to bring about the birth of the legendary King Arthur, and to be his magician. The story may be found in Geoffrey of Monmouth's *History of the Kings of Britain*.

Dolwyddelan

One mile from Dolwyddelan village, Gwynedd.

One of the castles of the princes of Gwynedd, Dolwyddelan, guards the pass that was once part of the track from the Vale of Conwy to Ardudwy. Although it has been claimed that it was the birthplace of Llywelyn ab Iorwerth, it is more likely that it was he who actually built this mountain fastness.

A two storey rectangular keep was surrounded by a hexagonal curtain wall which followed the contours of the rocky site. This was later strengthened by

Edward I of England after the fall of Gwynedd's royal house (see Aberedw and Castell y Bere).

Llywelyn ab Iorwerth, also known as Llywelyn Fawr or 'The Great', was born in around 1173, probably quite close to Dolwyddelan. Lord of Gwynedd and descendant of Owain Gwynedd and Gruffudd ap Cynan, Llywelyn was to prove a worthy successor to these formidable leaders.

Following the usual internal friction between the Welsh lords, he had succeeded in defeating his uncle Dafydd ab Owain and consolidating his hold on Gwynedd by 1200.

Llywelyn swore fealty to the English king John, and was known as Prince of North Wales, but his position was not entirely secure. Throughout his long reign he had to fight off rivals, both Welsh and English. He built a number of castles in order to strengthen his position such as those at Castell y Bere, Cricieth, Ewloe and Dolbadarn, not far from Dolwyddelan. He needed them, too. John was alarmed at Llywelyn's increasing power. An army composed of John's English troops and rival Welsh lords such as Gruffudd ap Gwenwynwyn of Powys and Rhys Gryg of Deheubarth marched into Gwynedd in the summer of 1211. Llywelyn operated a scorched earth policy, so that the invaders would find no supplies on their route. Soon they were reduced to eating their horses, although it seems unlikely that the king would have to eat his mount. Any English-speakers in the King's army – for bear in mind that French was the language of the 'English' nobility at this time – may have found Rhys Gryg's nickname – which means Rhys the Hoarse – an appropriate one under the circumstances. The king's army was forced to retreat, but returned in the autumn. Llywelyn was forced to surrender, and had to pay a fine of 20,000 head of cattle to John. This was a very heavy price.

Llywelyn was a politician as well as a soldier, and showed this by marrying Joan or Siwan, illegitimate daughter of king John of England, in 1205. Joan was a useful intermediary with the English court, and she played a prominent part in the negotiations following Llywelyn's defeat of 1211. Although this was a political match, genuine affection does seem to have developed between them.

The course of true politics seldom runs smooth, however. One of Llywelyn's later struggles was with William Marshall, the powerful English noble. Marshall was drawn into strife between some of his own supporters and Llywelyn. During the fighting William de Braose, lord of Builth, was captured and held at Llywelyn's court at Aber. Llywelyn returned unexpectedly one day to discover de Braose in a rather compromising position with Joan. He was swiftly hanged.

Despite occasional setbacks, Llywelyn managed to maintain a substantial power base in North Wales. He was determined that this should pass on to just one of his sons in its entirety, rather than being split as was the usual Welsh custom. Llywelyn could see how many Welsh lords and princes had patiently struggled and worked in order to build up their power and territory, only for the inheritance to be lost in squabbles and infighting between their heirs. In 1238, therefore, at a conference in Strata Florida, Dafydd ap Llywelyn was recognised as his father's heir by the leading Welsh lords, who swore fealty to him. Llywelyn's other son, Gruffudd, was not to inherit.

After Llywelyn's death in 1240 he was succeeded by his son Dafydd who ruled for 6 years to 1246. Dafydd had no children to inherit, so the principality passed to the children of Gruffudd, who was already dead. It was left to Llywelyn ap Iorwerth's grandson Llywelyn, the son of Gruffudd, to build up an effective power base once again in Gwynedd.

Dolforwyn

One mile west of Abermule, near Newtown, Powys.

Dolforwyn is one of the castles that played a vital role in the story of Llywelyn ap Gruffydd, last native Prince of Wales. This was the only one of Llywelyn's own castles to be built entirely by the prince as a new foundation, and was started in 1273.

Llywelyn had wrung a number of concessions out of Edward I in the Treaty of Montgomery in 1267, including the right to call himself Prince of Wales, and he obviously felt confident enough to assert himself by building a new castle and borough. That he was to build his castle near the English-held stronghold of Montgomery added insult to Edward's injury. Edward was not amused, and informed Llywelyn of his extreme displeasure. It is a reflection of the importance attached to castles that monarchs were so quick to anger when an inconvenient fortification was built.

Llywelyn also wished to build a borough, or town, near the castle. This had more than just military implications – a town with a market became the centre of trade for the nearby countryside, and could bring in revenues to its lord. Many of the market towns within Wales at this time were dominated by English castles and traders – a process which was to accelerate greatly following Llywelyn's death.

Nothing daunted, Llywelyn defied Edward and his minions, claiming that 'the rights of our principality are entirely separate from the rights of your kingdom…' The Prince visited his new castle in Easter 1274, where he held court and asserted his power over the local Welsh lords.

The building of Dolforwyn was one of Edward I's pretexts for declaring Llywelyn a rebel in 1267. The English campaign, which lasted just under a year, was characteristically well planned and successful. Edward created three military commands, based on Chester, Montgomery and Carmarthen. The commanders of the English forces worked inwards towards Llywelyn's power base in Gwynedd.

Dolforwyn, Llywelyn's pride and joy, surrendered to the Earl of Lincoln and Roger Mortimer on 8 April 1277 because of a lack of water. The siege had taken just eight days. Further Welsh losses followed quickly. By the time that Edward appeared in person at Chester in July of that year, Llywelyn's forces had been soundly defeated.

The Prince of Wales lost much of the territory that he had gained at Montgomery a decade before, and was forced to come to humiliating terms with Edward in the Treaty of Aberconwy. Amongst other terms, Llywelyn had to pay a fine of £50,000 for his 'disobedience'. To give some idea of the size of that sum, Dolforwyn castle itself had cost some £174 to build. The native Welsh felt much resentment. The stage was now set for the final acts of this story – acts which would also involve many Welsh castles.

Aberedw and Builth castles

Aberedw, three miles south-east of Builth Wells. Builth castle is in the town itself.
The story of these two castles is closely intertwined. They lie within a few miles of each other in mid Wales, and were important in the story of Llywelyn ap Gruffudd.

Aberedw was one of Llywelyn's seats, although he may have owned Hen Gastell, the nearby ditched motte which once supported a tower. It is probable that the present Aberedw castle was fortified by Walter Hakelutel. The base of a round tower may be seen here, with traces of part of the inner wall and other towers. This Walter was a supporter of Edward Mortimer, who himself had an important role in Llywelyn's life.

Dafydd ap Gruffudd, Llywelyn's brother, had co-operated with Edward I against his brother during the war of 1277. He was disappointed that he did not receive the rewards he considered his by right for his support of the king.

His resentment led to him turning his coat once again. On Palm Sunday 1282 Dafydd and his followers attacked the English stronghold at Hawarden in north-east Wales. The English commander, Roger Clifford, was captured, and the garrison slaughtered. Despite his brother's treacherous record, Llywelyn had to assume control of the uprising if he was to retain credibility as leader of the native Welsh, and indeed gained some initial successes.

By winter of that year, Llywelyn moved south with an army and is said to have set up his base at Aberedw. What exactly happened afterwards is unclear, as contemporary chroniclers hint at treachery. It may be that he was tricked into the area by promises of support from Edward Mortimer and his family.

Llywelyn sent most of his men to Brecon, retaining a handful of followers himself. On the Friday after the feast of St Nicholas, 11 December 1282, they were surprised by an English force on the banks of the Irfon stream near Cilmeri. There Llywelyn was mortally wounded, possibly by one Stephen de Frankton. The fallen prince was not immediately recognised, but when he was, his head was cut from his body and sent to Edward in Rhuddlan. His head was later sent to London, where, crowned with an ivy band in mockery of his princely pretensions, it was impaled on a stake outside the Tower of London.

The Welsh poets, such an integral part of medieval Welsh life, reflected the desolation felt by their countrymen. A number of moving elegies record their feelings:

> 'Do you not see that the stars have fallen?' wrote Gruffudd ab yr
> Ynad Goch, 'Do you not see that the world is ending? Ah God, that
> the sea would cover the land!'

This linking of the death of their prince to the most powerful forces in nature reveals how powerfully Llywelyn's death affected his followers.

His body was carried over the mountains by the monks of Abaty Cwm Hir, some six miles from Rhaeadr. There it was buried, perhaps under the High Altar. A modern stone marks this site today, and it is a place of pilgrimage for many who remember Llywelyn and his struggle to maintain an independent Welsh state. A standing stone has been erected at Cilmeri, which also attracts those following Llywelyn ap Gruffudd's story.

Interestingly, although these memorials to Llywelyn stand today, very little remains of the castle which Edward I built at nearby Builth Wells whilst consolidating his conquest. The masonry was robbed centuries ago, although the earthworks upon which it stood give an impression of its one-time strength. Look for Castle Street if you would like to find its site.

Castell y Bere

Llanfihangel-y-Pennant, seven miles south-east of Dolgellau, Gwynedd.

This castle, situated deep in the Cadair Idris Range, saw one of the last acts in the tragic drama of the Welsh Rebellion of 1282-3. Dafydd ap Gruffydd, Llywelyn's brother and the man who had instigated the rebellion with his attack on Hawarden during Easter 1282, sought refuge here from Edward I's invading armies.

The castle had been built by Llywelyn ap Iorwerth in 1221, probably after he quarrelled with his son Gruffydd. Llywelyn's architect had to contend with the formidable rock upon which it was built. The present buildings closely follow the site's craggy contours. Towers, ditches and drawbridges strengthened the curtain walls that surround the rather strangely shaped ward. Rocky outcrops abound underfoot. Several of the buildings were adorned with richly carved stonework, some of which may be seen in the National Museum of Wales in Cardiff. This isolated stronghold above the Dysynni valley was Dafydd's base as he attempted to keep the embers of Welsh resistance alight after Llywelyn's death in December 1282.

Edward continued his cautious advance into the Welsh heartland following Llywelyn's death, conquering Snowdonia during January and February 1283, setting up his headquarters in Aberconwy on the Gwynedd coast in March. The pressure increased on Dafydd's last major garrison at Castell y Bere until the soldiers could take no more, and they surrendered on 25 April. This was, to all intents and purposes, the end for Dafydd.

He tried to keep up the pretence of power, summoning further forces to his aid. That aid never came. The Welsh were a spent force. In June 1283 Dafydd was captured near the Royal Palace at Aber 'by men of his own tongue', as the *Brut* has it, and taken to Shrewsbury. There he was hanged until nearly dead, his innards drawn out and burnt before him and his body cut into quarters. A plaque in Shrewsbury commemorates Dafydd's gruesome end.

Following Dafydd's execution, the leaders of the North Wales cantrefs, or groups of a hundred settlements, were bound to keep the peace to the sum of £2000 – a lot of money at the time, of course. They were also threatened with excommunication from the Church if they rose again against their English conquerors. This would have meant that they could not receive Holy Communion, or be buried in consecrated ground such as churchyards, and was a terrible punishment for a devout Christian.

The Welsh were to suffer further in the wake of Llywelyn and Dafydd's deaths. The Statute of Rhuddlan, passed in 1284, effectively announced the annexation of Wales and did away with many of the native laws and traditions which had governed Welsh life for centuries.

Incidentally, Llywelyn ap Gruffydd had been excommunicated by the Archbishop of Canterbury for rising up against Edward I, although his body was secretly buried in the consecrated ground at Abaty Cwm Hir by monks loyal to him.

The rather steep climb up to Castell y Bere may be more arduous than the route to some Welsh castles, but the dramatic situation and atmospheric ruins make it worth the exertion, particularly when one remembers its important role in the history of Wales.

Caernarfon

Caernarfon Castle, Gwynedd.

One of the most impressive fortifications in Britain, and a World Heritage Site, Caernarfon Castle is a mighty monument to the English conquest of Wales. This was part of the chain of castles built by Edward I to consolidate his conquest after the deaths of Llywelyn ap Gruffudd in 1282 and of his brother Dafydd the year after.

Edward's reasoning was simple. He did not want to have to commit such massive efforts to the subjugation of Wales again, so he decided to ensure that the English maintained a stranglehold on the Welsh that could not be shaken off. The best way to do this was to build castles.

This was perhaps not the cheapest option, as castles were expensive to erect. They were, however, a tried and tested way of dominating and controlling a land and its people, and that was what Edward and the English wanted to do. Welsh castles such as those at Cricieth and Castell y Bere were repaired, and other fortresses built in the Marches. Huge royal castles were also planned. The construction process began very soon after the Welsh defeat.

Conwy was begun in March 1283, and Harlech and Caernarfon in June of the same year. Conwy was virtually finished by the end of 1287, and Harlech by 1289. These amazingly short construction times reflect the effort that Edward poured into the work. Almost every county in England had to send workmen to help with the king's new fortresses. Indeed, some 4,000 men worked at the three new sites in 1283-4. They all had to be housed and paid, and huge quantities of materials had to be procured. Edward's castle building project was indeed a massive undertaking.

He was fortunate that he had one of the greatest military architects of the Middle Ages in his service. James of St George came from Savoy and was familiar with the most up-to-date castle-building techniques. He was made Master of the King's Works in Wales, and ensured that his constructions took advantage of the natural strengths of the chosen sites.

Hugh 'the Wolf' of Avranches had built a motte and bailey castle at Caernarfon during early Norman incursions into Gwynedd, and Edward was to use the same site. Massive curtain walls and polygonal towers were built in stone of more than one colour, giving the distinctive banded effect that is to be seen to this day. This was a conscious attempt to echo the appearance of the walls of Constantinople, capital of the Eastern Roman empire. Edward was trying to link himself and his conquest with the power of Imperial Rome, particularly as the Welsh associated Caernarfon with *Macsen Wledig*, who left Britain in 383 AD to become Emperor of Rome.

The huge Eagle Tower, surmounted by carved stone eagles, obviously echoes the Roman past and also reflect the Welsh name for Snowdonia – *Eryri*, abode of the eagles. Caernarfon Castle was one of the fortresses that ringed that mountainous region, which had been the traditional Welsh stronghold and refuge in times of invasion. Once again the message was clear. The Welsh had been conquered, and were not to be allowed to forget it.

Ironically enough, the Welsh were not completely subdued, and the castle was not completed without a hitch. Madog ap Llywelyn and a number of his fellow Welsh lords rose in revolt in 1284 following particularly heavy tax demands from the English. Madog's forces breached the town walls, which had been built when the castle was started, and damaged much of the as yet uncompleted castle.

The rebellion was put down in 1285, however, and the castle was eventually completed. Its strength was to be tested during the rebellion of Owain Glyndŵr (see Sycharth), when it was besieged twice. In 1403 Owain and his French allies lost 300 men before its walls, and again in 1404 the Welsh were beaten back, this time by a garrison of only 28. That a castle of this size could be held by such a small force is testament to the military genius of Edward I and James of St George.

The external appearance of the castle today is very impressive. The two extensive wards are often compared to an hourglass because of their layout. The massive King's Gate is a formidable entrance, and the banded curtain walls, punctuated by Edward's polygonal towers, continue to excite the awe and wonder of its beholders. Edward would perhaps have been unimpressed by the sight of the Red Dragon of Cadwallader flying above his mighty fortification.

Dryslwyn

Five miles west of Llandeilo, Carmarthenshire, on the B4297.

Dryslwyn stands upon a steep hill near a major crossing of the river Tywi, and is clearly visible for miles around. It is first mentioned in 1245, and was probably built by one of Lord Rhys ap Gruffudd's descendants. In 1271 Maredudd ap Rhys of Deheubarth died within its walls.

This castle really came to prominence when Maredudd's son, Rhys ap Maredudd, rose in revolt against Edward I. Rhys and his father had loyally supported the kings of England against the Princes of Gwynedd for many years, but he felt hard done by the royal Justiciar of West Wales and the constable of nearby Dinefwr castle. Disillusioned, Rhys rose in revolt on June 8 1287.

The king responded with characteristic swiftness and efficiency. We have a letter from the king addressed to the Knights and all others of the counties of Salop and Stafford. He ordered them '...to assist with their horses, arms, and power Roger Lestrange, whom the king is sending to Wales to repress the rebellion of Rhys son of Mereduc and his accomplices, Welshmen.' Armies of over 24,000 men were raised within weeks.

Rhys found himself under siege in Dryslwyn later on in June. An army of 11,000 men under the command of Edward, Earl of Cornwall, surrounded the castle. They also brought up a trebuchet, a massive piece of equipment that was drawn by forty oxen over smooth ground, but needed sixty to pull it over rougher areas. It was protected by twenty horsemen and four hundred and eighty infantry. Twenty quarrymen made four hundred and eighty huge stone 'bullets' that were brought up by four carters as ammunition. The bill for fitting up the engine, and buying hides, timber, rope and lead came to £14.

Smaller engines were also used, but the use of undermining in an attempt to bring down the walls was a major element of the English attack. The mining and battering operations were in full swing between August 20th and 30th. Unfortunately for the attackers, the mine collapsed unexpectedly early. One hundred and fifty men, both miners and soldiers close to the wall at the time of the disaster, were killed, including one William de Montchensy.

Despite this setback for the attackers Rhys saw that his days would be numbered if he remained in the castle. He escaped through a postern and fled to Newcastle Emlyn, capturing that fortress by surprise. By the time that this stronghold fell in January, the elusive Rhys had decamped to Ireland. In the meanwhile, Dryslwyn had fallen in September. Rhys remained at large until he was betrayed in April 1292, when he was taken to York and executed. The ancient royal dynasty of Deheubarth, the lineage of Hywel Dda and Lord Rhys, effectively died with him.

A new borough was soon established near Dryslwyn and settled by English burgesses. The castle remained in royal control until the 15th century, although Owain Glyndŵr's forces captured it in 1403.

The remains of the inner ward and round keep may be seen today, with the outer ward on the ridge to the north-east. Bumps in the nearby turf reveal the location of part of the medieval borough.

Despite the steep climb up to the castle, this is a fine site, and a wonderful place for children to play – if properly supervised. Spare a thought for the besiegers as you toil up the hillside.

Beaumaris *Biwmares*

Beaumaris Castle, Anglesey.

The Norman-French name of this castle – *Beau Mareys*, the beautiful or fine marsh – hints at it's non-Welsh origins. This is in fact another of Edward I's castles, and another World Heritage Site. Edward left a very substantial architectural legacy indeed in Wales. He built or rebuilt Aberystwyth, Builth, Harlech, Caernarfon, Conwy, Rhuddlan, Flint and Hope castles. He also repaired Dryslwyn, Dinefwr, Castell y Bere, Cricieth, and Dolwyddelan. Edward's controlling hand may be detected at seventeen Welsh castles – with the master architect James of St George responsible for at least twelve of these. More castles were built, rebuilt or repaired by other English lords.

Altogether, then, there was a massive permanent English military presence in Wales, allied to the towns or boroughs built in the shadow of many castles – towns that were occupied by English and other non-Welsh settlers. Boroughs were built at Flint, Rhuddlan and Aberystwyth in 1277, and then at Conwy, Caernarfon and Harlech. Defences for these six fortified boroughs, also known as *bastides*, were integrated with those of the nearby castles.

The burgesses, or inhabitants of the boroughs, were vital to Edward's consolidation of his Welsh conquests. Many were ex-soldiers who could be relied upon both to fight and to produce new fighting men within their families. They could also perform economic functions and help provide for the needs of the castle's inhabitants.

This is illustrated in the Charter of Henry de Lacy given to Denbigh c.1300 which, although not a royal castle, also had a borough which fulfilled the same function as a royal foundation. We see that '… each of the burgesses… or the heirs of each of them being Englishmen, shall find an armed man in Denbigh for the guard and defence of the aforesaid town… ' Those who did not provide an armed man were to lose their property within the town.

A borough was built at Beaumaris too, although it was not to be fortified until 1414 during Owain Glyndŵr's revolt. Beaumaris Castle itself was instigated as yet another link in Edward's chain of stone following the Welsh revolt of 1294–5 led by Madog ap Llywelyn. The site was chosen to command one end of the Menai straits which separate Anglesey from the mainland, with Caernarfon covering the other. The open site gave James of St George the room to build a perfect concentric castle. As a result Beaumaris is a world-famous example of classic concentric design.

In common with the other Edwardian castles, its building was a massive undertaking. According to Master James himself, 'the work… is very costly and we need a great deal of money'. This may be familiar to those of us who have had dealings with builders during more recent times. Approximately 2,000 labourers, 400 masons, and thirty blacksmiths and carpenters started work there in the summer of 1295.

Something that may also strike a chord with modern readers is that Beaumaris was never quite finished, despite the enormous amount of resources poured into it – although it was rated as being defensible by 1298. Two wards were built one within the other on a concentric plan, with the curtain walls punctuated by substantial gatehouses and round towers. The outer ward was enclosed by a water-filled moat. Its walls were, of course, lower than the inner so that missiles could be fired from both lines of defence simultaneously. The gatehouses were very strong, but were also to provide extensive and comfortable living apartments – although they were never made as luxurious as originally planned. Building took a long time, too, continuing at least until 1330 – during the reign of Edward III, Edward I's grandson.

Nevertheless, the fortifications incorporated virtually every nasty trick in the castle builder's repertoire. The walls were, of course, crenellated and machicolated, with portcullises (iron or wooden gratings within the gatehouses, which could be let down to bar the gateway or to trap attackers) and murder holes. The castle even had a little fortified dock on the Menai straits, which could supply it by sea. It was a formidable fortress indeed.

It needed to be formidable, as continued Welsh hostility to the English meant that defence was important for many years. As Master James wrote in 1296, 'Welshmen are Welshmen, and you need to understand them properly; if… there is war with France and Scotland, we shall need to watch them all the more closely.'

The truth of this was to be demonstrated during Glyndŵr's rebellion, when the Welsh held it for two years. It also saw action until the English Revolution, when it was refortified by royalist forces under the nearby landowner Richard Bulkely of Baron Hill. In 1648 it fell to the Parliamentarians who garrisoned it for several years after the war. It is said that a Royalist officer foresaw defeat during the siege and ran away, locking his men in the Church tower. He was swiftly nicknamed Captain Church.

The castle today is in a pretty good state of repair, with the classic concentric design clearly visible. It houses interesting exhibitions explaining the castle's historical context. The town of Beaumaris is itself very popular with tourists. All in all a good place to reflect on the architectural genius of Master James of St George, and on Edward I's military might.

Caerffili

Caerffili Castle.

It is hard to miss Caerffili Castle. It dominates its surroundings, unsurprisingly as it is the largest castle in Wales and twice the size of the Tower of London. Perhaps surprisingly, considering its great size, this was not a royal fortress, but was begun in 1268 by Gilbert 'the Red' de Clare, earl of Gloucester and Lord of Glamorgan, near the site of a Roman fort.

De Clare had become alarmed by the growing support that Llywelyn ap Gruffudd was receiving from the Welsh lords of upland Glamorgan, and particularly by his encroachments in Breconshire which borders Glamorgan. The earl imprisoned Gruffudd ap Rhys, lord of Senghennydd, and stole his lands. These included Caerffili, where de Clare commenced work on a new fortress. Unfortunately for de Clare, Llywelyn attacked and demolished the new castle in any case. Once Llywelyn became distracted by his struggles with Edward I, however, de Clare carried on with his works at Caerffili, which was to become the first concentric castle in Britain.

Gilbert's son, also Gilbert, was killed at the battle of Bannockburn in 1314, and the castle passed to Gilbert's granddaughter, Eleanor, and her husband Hugh le Despenser, a favourite of king Edward II. Despite a poor harvest in 1315 the custodian of Glamorgan, Payn de Turberville, continued to squeeze unreasonable rents from the poverty-stricken Welsh. All sections of Glamorgan's native Welsh society had been alienated to such a degree that a revolt encompassed the whole of the lordship of Glamorgan, both Welsh and English, during January–March 1316. The revolt was led by Llywelyn ap Gruffudd, better known as Llywelyn Bren of Gelligaer, son of the dispossessed Lord of Senghennydd. He had taken his complaints of oppression to the English king but, like Owain Glyndŵr after him, received no satisfaction.

Llywelyn's men besieged Caerffili but could make little impression upon the formidable defences. The king and his nobles raised an army to suppress the revolt and Llywelyn realised that he was fighting a battle that he could not win, and that continuing the fighting would harm his people further. He and his two sons surrendered themselves to the English forces at Castell Coch, Ystradfellte in the bleak hills of Breconshire on March 18. They and Lleucu, Llywelyn's wife, were imprisoned in the Tower of London at the king's command.

Hugh le Despenser then took Llywelyn into custody, and in 1318 he was hung, drawn and quartered in Cardiff. Interestingly, the native Welsh were not the only ones to feel disgust at this treatment – a number of the English Marcher Lords also criticised le Despenser's barbarity. It seems that even they could see that Llywelyn and the people of Glamorgan had been pushed too far by unreasonable demands. Indeed, Humphrey de Bohun of Hereford was to receive the widowed Lleucu into his care, and was to give her small sums of money until 1349, when she is presumed to have died.

Le Despenser himself was to come to a sticky end in 1326 when he and the king were hunted down by a coalition of nobles. Despenser was hanged, and Edward II, who was captured near Llantrisant in Glamorgan, humiliated and barbarically murdered in Berkeley Castle.

The castle gradually decayed over the centuries, with much stone being robbed for building purposes. The Marquesses of Bute restored the castle during the 19th and 20th centuries, although they left one of the towers leaning at a precarious angle This may either be a casualty of the English Revolution, or, rather less dramatically, of subsidence.

Caerffili Castle's massive walls and water defences present a formidable aspect even today, and justifiably draw large numbers of tourists every year.

Sycharth

On private land, near Llangedwyn, Powys.

Little remains of Sycharth. The site, just beyond a farmhouse, comprises of earthworks that reveal the one-time presence of a motte and bailey castle, and not a particularly strong one at that. This is an important and interesting site, however, for a number of reasons. Firstly, we have a wonderful poetic description of Sycharth during its heyday in the 14th and 15th centuries. Secondly this was the home of Owain Glyndŵr, Prince of Wales.

Owain was one of the *uchelwyr*, a class of nobles that developed in Wales following the Edwardian conquest. His father was Gruffudd Fychan ap Madog, baron of Glyndyfrdwy and Cynllaith Owain in north-east Wales and a descendant of the kings of Powys. Owain's mother was Helen, daughter of Thomas Llywelyn ab Owain, descended from the royal line of Deheubarth. Royal blood therefore flowed in Owain's veins.

Born around 1350, he studied in London and later served the English king, quite typically for a Welsh noble of this period. He fought with Richard II in Scotland in 1385 and 1387, and later returned to the estates that he inherited from his father. With his main seat at Sycharth he lived the comfortable life of a wealthy *uchelwr*. There were a number of itinerant bards or poets travelling around Wales at this time,

Owain Glyndŵr

men of high status who effectively sang for their supper, producing poems which often praised the bounty of their patrons or hosts. They were the newspapermen and spin-doctors of their time, spreading information and gathering intelligence across the country.

One such poet was Iolo Goch, whose '*Llys Owain Glyndŵr yn Sycharth*', Owain Glyndŵr's court at Sycharth, describes the building and grounds, and the generosity of his host. We therefore have a picture of the house of a wealthy uchelwr during this period.

The house itself, a splendid wooden hall with a tiled roof, was built on the motte. A bridge connected the motte with the bailey with its lesser buildings. Nearby were orchards, vineyards, a rabbit warren, a deer park, fishponds, a mill and excellent farmland. There were herons and peacocks – which were eaten then, of course – and white bread, which was not common fare at the time, was eaten in the house. There were wines and spirits, beer and mead. Most importantly for Iolo and his bardic colleagues, wandering poets were always welcome here. Indeed,

> *Na gwall, na newyn, na gwarth,*
> *Na syched fyth yn Sycharth*
> (No want, no hunger, no shame,
> Nor thirst are ever at Sycharth)

High praise indeed. Even if Iolo was exaggerating a little, Owain must have enjoyed a very comfortable lifestyle. Why, then, did he risk all this, and rise up against the English throne?

Although Owain and his fellow *uchelwyr* co-operated with their English conquerors, it does not seem that they were afforded parity of esteem with neighbouring English nobles. Welsh noblemen and churchmen did not generally attain high office, although they did not suffer as much economically as the ordinary peasants. There was an awareness of the difference between native Welsh and incomers, and a feeling that the incomers were more privileged than the native people.

When Owain entered into a land dispute with Reginald Grey, lord of nearby Rhuthun, he failed to gain satisfaction through the English legal system.

When warned that the Welsh were increasingly dissatisfied by such attitudes, Parliament's response was 'What care we for these bare foot rascals?'. Owain had had enough. On 16 September 1400 he was declared Prince of Wales, and Welshmen flocked to his banner. Although his cause flourished for a time, and his enemy Grey was captured, ultimately he could not withstand English military might. In May 1403 Prince Henry, later to become Henry V, put Glyndyfrdwy and Sycharth to the torch. Its splendours were gone forever, although Owain fought on.

Very little remains at Sycharth now. There is little to inform the casual traveller that this was once the focal point of a fledgling Welsh princedom. Nevertheless, when we read Iolo Goch's lines, it is possible to return for a while to Glyndŵr's noble house.

You may not go quite as far as George Borrow, however, who chanted a translation of Iolo's poem while he sat upon the motte in 1854 which he had made many years before, then covered his face with his hands and wept for his lost innocence. Borrow's travels took him near a number of castles and historical sites, and his work, *Wild Wales*, is rightly considered a classic of its kind.

An important place in Welsh history, and one which deserves wider recognition.

Harlech

Harlech Castle, Gwynedd.

One of the most splendid and evocative Welsh castles, and a World Heritage site, Harlech dominates the surrounding landscape from its rocky crag. Although now inland this precipitous eminence once stood right on the seashore. It is said that the giant Welsh king Bendigeidfran, Brân the Blessed, looked out from here and saw the approaching sails of Matholwch, king of Ireland. The Irish king was coming to Wales in pursuit of the hand of Branwen, Brân's sister. This legend may be found in the *Mabinogi,* the Welsh tales that are one of the glories of medieval European literature.

Harlech was one of the mighty fortresses built by Edward I following the death of Llywelyn ap Gruffudd in 1282. Edward intended to encircle and control the traditional Welsh stronghold and refuge of Snowdonia, and the construction of Harlech, Conwy and Caernarfon was central to his strategy. This followed the success of Builth, Aberystwyth, Flint and Rhuddlan castles, built after the war of 1277. These had withstood Welsh attacks in 1282, and were valuable bases from which counter-attacks had been launched. The master mason, James of St George, took charge of construction at Harlech and was constable of the castle from 1290 to 1293.

This castle is notable for one of this master mason's innovations – the role of the substantial gatehouse as a comfortable residence as well as a formidable defensive structure. The curtain walls and towers show how powerful a fortress this was. An interesting feature along the southern curtain wall is the site of the relocated Ystumgwern Hall. This had been the hall of Llywelyn ap Gruffudd, and was moved to Harlech from its site some four miles away early in the fourteenth century. This was a symbolic gesture as much as anything – Llywelyn's hall was dwarfed by the massive structure surrounding it, and it was patently obvious who was the victor in the power struggle that had taken place. The castle cost some £9,000 to build – a colossal sum.

Harlech was to play a part in further struggles. It held out against Madog ab Llywelyn in 1294, with provisions arriving by sea, but a more serious challenge was to come. Having risen against the English and defeating them at the battle of Hyddgen in 1401, Owain Glyndŵr had to attack their castles. Conwy fell to him on Good Friday 1401. The nobles Reginald Grey and Edward Mortimer were captured in 1402. The Welsh were victorious in battle at Pilleth, to the north of Radnor, in June of that year, and English expeditions into Wales were largely unsuccessful. Owain's rebellion spread into South Wales, and he was soon to forge links with the Percy family, earls of Northumberland. An alliance with France bore fruit, as French and Breton forces helped at the siege of Kidwelly in October. A French fleet attacked the castle and town of Caernarfon in November. Owain's revolt had attained European significance.

In 1404, after a long siege, Owain's men captured Harlech Castle. This was the high point of the rebellion. Owain made Harlech his capital, and held at least one Parliament there. Soon more French soldiers landed at Haverfordwest, marched inland, took Carmarthen town and carried on nearly to Worcester. It seemed that Owain's ideals – a Welsh government, Welsh universities, and a free Welsh Church – were on the verge of becoming reality. It was not to last.

The rebellion ran out of momentum by 1408. The English kings defeated the Percies, the French alliance collapsed in 1407, and Owain had to rely on his own resources. They were not sufficient to withstand the wealth and military might of England. Harlech fell to the English in 1408, and Owain's wife, daughter and four grandchildren were captured. Although pockets of rebellion were still to be found for some years – into the 1420s – Owain's power was broken and his rebellion effectively over. Wales was to take many years to recover from the devastation caused by both sides during Glyndŵr's revolt.

Although he was never captured, it is thought that he may have stayed with his daughter and her husband at Monnington Court in what is now Herefordshire. Perhaps there, just over the border in present day England, he died and was buried. Other legends claim that, like that other Welshman, Arthur, Glyndŵr is just sleeping, waiting for a time of great need before he may rise again.

Montgomery *Trefaldwyn*

Above Montgomery town, Powys.

Montgomery, yet another fortress perched on high ground above a town, commands the Severn valley. It was built by Henry III between 1223 and 1234 to replace the nearby motte and bailey known now as 'Hen Domen' or old mound. Hen Domen had been built in 1071 by Roger de Montgommerie, who gave his name to the castle and town.

Henry built his new fortress in an attempt to frustrate Llywelyn ap Iorwerth's territorial ambitions in the area. Indeed, Llywelyn burnt the castle and nearby town in 1228. The fortress was rebuilt and strengthened, and was to become a very formidable stronghold. It was further strengthened in response to the building of Dolforwyn Castle, a mere five miles away, by Llywelyn ap Gruffydd.

After the fall of the Princes of Gwynedd, Montgomery was no longer a front line fortress, and passed into the hands of the Mortimer family during the 15th century. They added domestic buildings such as a bakehouse and brewhouse, reflecting the rather more settled and peaceful times and the new emphasis on convenience and comfort.

Lord Herbert of nearby Chirbury became owner of the castle and built a brick house in the middle ward in 1622. He obviously felt that defence was no longer a priority. This was not to last long, however, as the English Revolution or Civil War was on the horizon. Herbert garrisoned the castle, but took fright when the Parliamentarian Sir Thomas Middleton appeared outside his walls with about 800 foot- and horsemen on Wednesday 4 September 1644.

According to a contemporary account, the gallant Herbert agreed to pay a large sum of money to the besiegers in order to free himself, his tenants and neighbours from plunder, and his castle from siege. He also agreed to discharge some of his garrison.

However, Lieutenant Colonel James Till, 'accompanied by strong forces, and having a petard [mine or bomb] with him, came into the gates of the castle upon Thursday night about twelve, and causing a trumpet to be sounded, required that the castle be "presently" yielded'.

Upon this, Herbert demanded that they retreat as, according to the terms of their agreement, 'their business was deferred until next morning'. Till, nothing daunted, 'affirming he had a petard, gave that terror to Lord Herbert's servants and garrison that some leaped over the wall'.

Although Herbert demanded that Till retreat once again, the Colonel stood firm. Herbert had to enter into a treaty with him, under conditions later agreed by Middleton. The preceding quotations come from Till's own account of the siege, which he wrote with Captain Samuel More, as published during the last century.

Middleton later interceded on Herbert's behalf before Parliament, stating that the noble lord had, in effect, kept his head down and not been a particularly fervent supporter of the king, 'and has done nothing to offend Parliament'. This meant that he should keep his land and property. Herbert was also given a safe conduct addressed to the governors of territory on his way to London, whence he retired 'for his health'.

A Royalist force attacked the castle and it's new Parliamentarian garrison, but was driven off on 18th September by Middleton's relief force which left 400 Royalists dead and took fourteen hundred prisoners. This was the greatest battle of the first Civil War in Wales. Middleton went on to destroy royal power in North Wales during this campaign.

He was also to find himself in the unusual position of besieging his own castle at Chirk. Middleton was also to switch sides and fight for the Royalists – perhaps an unwise move in view of the eventual victors, although his son was eventually made a baronet by the restored Charles II. The ways of fate are indeed obscure.

The 1644 'Certificate of the Losses of Lord Herbert and the Inhabitants of the Town of Mountgomery upon the Surrender of Mountgomery Castle' claims that the depredations of the King's and Parliament's armies led to a loss of £4,940 14s 0d for Herbert, and £3,066 12s 10d for the inhabitants of the town. War was an expensive business.

Although Herbert was to continue his protestations of innocence to Parliament, Montgomery Castle was slighted, and later demolished in 1649.

Montgomery today is a fine example of a border town, with picturesque and peaceful surroundings which belie its troubled history.

Picton Castle *Castell Pictwn*

Three miles south-east of Haverfordwest, Pembrokeshire.

The first castle on this site was built by William de Picton during the reign of William II or William Rufus. The present remains date from the 13th–14th centuries. The core of the castle is a solid block with four round towers, probably built by Sir John Wogan, Justiciar of Ireland under Edward I.

Picton was captured by Glyndŵr's forces in 1405, and was captured twice during the English Revolution – by the Royalists in 1643, and then by Parliamentary soldiers in 1645.

During this second siege Sir Richard Philipps held the castle for the king. It was a long drawn out affair, and was brought to an end, it is said, when a hostage was captured in a rather unusual way.

The castle nursery was situated in one of the lower rooms, and had a window looking outwards. A nursemaid was looking after the baby Erasmus Phillipps in this room when she saw a Parliamentarian messenger approaching under a flag of truce. She opened the window and leaned out in order to receive the message. The messenger, seeing his chance, grabbed the baby and rode back to his camp as fast as his horse's legs could carry him.

The garrison was offered an ultimatum – surrender the castle or sacrifice the child. They surrendered immediately. Perhaps impressed by the Royalists' honourable behaviour – and perhaps in the light of their own rather opportunistic and doubtful tactics – the castle's garrison was allowed the full honours of war, and the castle itself was spared from slighting.

Picton has been altered, and has become a comfortable dwelling. Although it remains in private hands, many rooms are open to the public in the summer. It also houses an art gallery, and is surrounded by attractive gardens.

Saint Fagan's *Sain Ffagan*

Four miles west of Cardiff.

Little may now be seen of the medieval castle that stood on this site. The remaining sections of curtain wall probably date from the 13th century, and it may be that part of the keep was incorporated into the Elizabethan mansion which now stands here. This sequence illustrates how post-medieval landowners felt able to abandon the safety of their uncomfortable old castles in favour of more luxurious, if less defensible, dwellings, as times became safer and less violent.

The history of St Fagan's illustrates how such faith in the tranquillity of the times was misplaced, as the largest battle of the English Revolution or Civil war that took place in Wales was fought nearby.

John Poyer, the Parliamentarian governor of Pembroke castle, had refused to hand over that fortress to a detachment of Cromwell's New Model Army unless arrears of pay were given to him and his men. As time went on his frustration became allied with personal animosity towards neighbours of his who claimed that he was less than honest in his financial dealings. The put-upon Poyer worried that 'men of blood' now 'thirsted after' his life.

Poyer cracked and declared for King Charles on 10 April 1648. He was joined by Rice Powell and Rowland Laugharne, both former Parliamentary supporters who turned against Cromwell and his generals. They marched an army of some 8,000 poorly armed and ill-trained men across South Wales until they encountered 3,000 battle-hardened and well-disciplined Parliamentary Ironsides at St Fagan's under the command of Colonel Horton on May 8 of that year. Although heavily outnumbered, Horton's men put their training and superior weaponry to good use. Two hundred of the Royalist forces were killed, and 3,000 captured. The three ringleaders scurried back into Pembrokeshire, pursued by Horton and his avenging Ironsides, and soon by Cromwell himself.

Powell had gone to ground in Tenby, which he surrendered unconditionally to Horton on 31 May. The paranoid Poyer was meanwhile holed up in Pembroke Castle, boasting of his bravery and resolve. Cromwell laid siege, but knew that the mighty medieval walls were still a formidable obstacle to any attacker. An attempt to starve out the intransigent garrison failed after Cromwell's men were reduced to virtually starvation rations themselves. However, Poyer had to surrender on 11 July when threatened with heavy guns and mortars which the castle could not withstand, and which had had to be transported by sea from Gloucester.

Cromwell was to show more restraint and mercy in Pembrokeshire than he was late to exhibit in Ireland. Laugharne, Powell and Poyer were condemned to death, but it was decreed that only one should die. The unfortunate Poyer drew the fatal lot, and was shot at Covent Garden on 25 April 1649.

St Fagan's today seems a world away from such tumultuous times. The mansion and grounds now house the justly renowned Museum of Welsh Life. The mansion houses furniture and other exhibits reflecting its long history, whilst historic buildings from all over Wales have been carefully moved here and painstakingly re-erected. Visitors to St Fagan's may see for themselves how Welsh people lived and worked over the centuries.

Book List

This is not a comprehensive bibliography. Many books deal with castles in general, and others specifically with Welsh Castles. Many more deal with the history of Wales. This is a selection. Titles with an asterisk (*) are part of a series of books on a similar theme, all of which may not be mentioned here.

Gazetteers of Welsh castles
Castles of Breconshire, Paul Remfry, 1999*
Cestyll Ceredigion, Afan ab Alun, 1991
The Castles of Mid Wales, Mike Salter, 1991*
The Castles of South-West Wales, Mike Salter, 1996*
The Castles of Wales, Alan Reid, 1998
The Castles of Wales, Lindsay Evans, 1998
Wales – Castles and Historic Places, D M Robinson and R S Thomas

Welsh History
A History of Wales, John Davies, 1993
Famous Welsh Battles, Philip Warner, 1977
Llywelyn ap Gruffudd, J B Smith, 1986
Medieval Wales, David Walker, 1990
Stuart Wales, W S K Thomas, 1988*
The Age of Conquest – Wales 1063–1415, R R Davies, 1991*
Yr Arglwydd Rhys, gol. N A Jones a H Pryce, 1996

Contemporary Sources mentioned in this book:

Herbert Correspondence, ed. W J Smith, 1963
Llywelyn y Beirdd, gol. J E Caerwyn Williams, E Rolant, Alan Llwyd, 1984
The History of the Kings of Britain, Geoffrey of Monmouth, trans. Lewis Thorpe, 1966

The Journey through Wales/The Description of Wales, Gerald of Wales, trans. Lewis Thorpe 1978

Wild Wales, George Borrow, 1862 and later editions

Yr Oesoedd Canol, Rhan 1, M B Evans, 1973*

Yr Oesoedd Canol, Rhan 2, M B Evans, 1978*

– Wales within your reach:
an attractive series
at attractive prices!

1. Welsh Talk
Heini Gruffudd
086243 447 5
£2.95

2. Welsh Dishes
Rhian Williams
086243 492 0
£2.95

3. Welsh Songs
Lefi Gruffudd (ed.)
086243 525 0
£3.95

4. Welsh Mountain Walks
Dafydd Andrews
086243 547 1
£3.95

5. Welsh Organic Recipes
Dave and Barbara Frost
086243 574 9
£3.95

6. Welsh Railways
Jim Green
086243 551 X
£3.95

7. Welsh Place Names
Brian Davies
086243 514 5
£3.95

8. Welsh Castles
Geraint Roberts
086243 550 1
£3.95

9. Welsh Rugby Heroes
Androw Bennett
086243 552 8
£3.95

Also to be published in the *It's Wales* series:

Welsh National Heroes

Welsh History

Welsh Jokes

The *It's Wales* series
is just one of a wide range
Welsh interest publications
from Y Lolfa.
For a full list of books currently in print,
send now for your free copy
of our new, full-colour Catalogue
– or simply surf into our website
at **www.ylolfa.com.**

Talybont Ceredigion Cymru/*Wales* SY24 5AP
ffôn 0044 (0)1970 832 304   *ffacs* 832 782   *isdn* 832 813
e-bost ylolfa@ylolfa.com   *y we* www.ylolfa.com